MW01025397

A COUNTRY IS NOT
A COMPANY

Harvard Business Review

CLASSICS

A COUNTRY IS NOT A COMPANY

Paul Krugman

Harvard Business Press
Boston, Massachusetts

Copyright 2009 Harvard Business School Publishing Corporation

Originally published in *Harvard Business Review* in January 1996

Reprint 96108

All rights reserved

Printed in the United States of America

No part of this publication may be reproduced, stored in or introduced into a retrieval system, or transmitted, in any form, or by any means (electronic, mechanical, photocopying, recording, or otherwise), without the prior permission of the publisher. Requests for permission should be directed to permissions@hbsp. harvard.edu, or mailed to Permissions, Harvard Business School Publishing, 60 Harvard Way, Boston, Massachusetts 02163.

ISBN: 978-1-63369-502-3

Library-of-Congress cataloging information forthcoming

THE HARVARD BUSINESS
REVIEW CLASSICS SERIES

Since 1922, *Harvard Business Review* has been a leading source of breakthrough ideas in management practice—many of which still speak to and influence us today. The HBR Classics series now offers you the opportunity to make these seminal pieces a part of your permanent management library. Each volume contains a groundbreaking idea that has shaped best practices and inspired countless managers around the world—and will change how you think about the business world today.

A COUNTRY IS NOT
A COMPANY

College students who plan to go into business often major in economics, but few believe that they will end up using what they hear in the lecture hall. Those students understand a fundamental truth: What they learn in economics courses won't help them run a business.

The converse is also true: What people learn from running a business won't help them formulate economic policy. A country is not a big corporation. The habits of mind that make a great business leader are not, in general, those that make a great economic analyst; an executive who has made $1 billion is rarely the right person to turn to for advice about a $6 trillion economy.

Why should that be pointed out? After all, neither businesspeople nor economists are usually very good poets, but so what? Yet many people (not least successful business executives themselves) believe that someone who has made a personal fortune will know how to make an entire nation more prosperous. In fact, his or her advice is often disastrously misguided.

I am not claiming that businesspeople are stupid or that economists are particularly smart. On the contrary, if the 100 top U.S.

business executives got together with the 100 leading economists, the least impressive of the former group would probably outshine the most impressive of the latter. My point is that the style of thinking necessary for economic analysis is very different from that which leads to success in business. By understanding that difference, we can begin to understand what it means to do good economic analysis and perhaps even help some businesspeople become the great economists they surely have the intellect to be.

Let me begin with two examples of economic issues that I have found business executives generally do not understand: first, the relationship between exports and job creation, and, second, the relationship

between foreign investment and trade
balances. Both issues involve international
trade, partly because it is the area I know
best but also because it is an area in which
businesspeople seem particularly inclined to
make false analogies between countries and
corporations.

EXPORTS AND JOBS

Business executives consistently misunder-
stand two things about the relationship
between international trade and domestic job
creation. First, since most U.S. businesspeople support free trade, they generally agree
that expanded world trade is good for world
employment. Specifically, they believe that

free trade agreements such as the recently concluded General Agreement on Tariffs and Trade are good largely because they mean more jobs around the world. Second, businesspeople tend to believe that countries compete for those jobs. The more the United States exports, the thinking goes, the more people we will employ, and the more we import, the fewer jobs will be available. According to that view, the United States must not only have free trade but also be sufficiently competitive to get a large proportion of the jobs that free trade creates.

Do those propositions sound reasonable? Of course they do. This sort of rhetoric dominated the last U.S. presidential election and will likely be heard again in the upcoming

race. However, economists in general do
not believe that free trade creates more
jobs worldwide (or that its benefits should
be measured in terms of job creation) or
that countries that are highly successful
exporters will have lower unemployment
than those that run trade deficits.

Why don't economists subscribe to
what sounds like common sense to businesspeople? The idea that free trade means more
global jobs seems obvious: More trade
means more exports and therefore more
export-related jobs. But there is a problem
with that argument. Because one country's
exports are another country's imports, every
dollar of export sales is, as a matter of sheer
mathematical necessity, matched by a dollar

of spending shifted from some country's domestic goods to imports. Unless there is some reason to think that free trade will increase total world spending—which is not a necessary outcome—overall world demand will not change.

Moreover, beyond this indisputable point of arithmetic lies the question of what limits the overall number of jobs available. Is it simply a matter of insufficient demand for goods? Surely not, except in the very short run. It is, after all, easy to increase demand. The Federal Reserve can print as much money as it likes, and it has repeatedly demonstrated its ability to create an economic boom when it wants to. Why, then, doesn't the Fed try to keep the economy booming all the time? Because it believes, with good reason, that if it were to do so—if it were to create too many jobs—the result would be unacceptable and accelerating inflation. In other words, the constraint on the number of jobs in the United States is not the U.S. economy's ability to generate demand, from exports or any other source, but the level of unemployment that the Fed thinks the economy needs in order to keep inflation under control.

That is not an abstract point. During 1994, the Fed raised interest rates seven times and made no secret of the fact that it was doing so to cool off an economic boom that it feared would create too many jobs, overheat the economy, and lead to inflation. Consider what that implies for the effect of trade on employment. Suppose that the U.S. economy were to experience an export surge. Suppose, for example, that the United States agreed to drop its objections to slave labor if China agreed to buy $200 billion worth of U.S. goods. What would the Fed do? It would offset the expansionary effect of the exports by raising interest rates; thus any increase in export-related jobs would be more or less matched by a loss of jobs in interest-rate-sensitive sectors of the economy, such as construction. Conversely, the Fed would surely respond to an import surge by lowering interest rates, so the direct loss of jobs to import competition would be roughly matched by an increased number of jobs elsewhere.

Even if we ignore the point that free trade always increases world imports by exactly as much as it increases world exports, there is still no reason to expect free trade to increase U.S. employment, nor should we expect any other trade policy, such as export promotion, to increase the total number of jobs in our economy. When the U.S. secretary of commerce returns from a trip abroad with billions of dollars in new orders for U.S. companies, he may or may not be instrumental in creating thousands of export-related jobs. If he is, he is also instrumental in destroying a roughly equal number of jobs elsewhere in the economy. The ability of the U.S. economy to increase exports or roll back imports has essentially nothing to do with its success in creating jobs.

Needless to say, this argument does not sit well with business audiences. (When I argued on one business panel that the North American Free Trade Agreement would have no effect, positive or negative, on the total number of jobs in the United States, one of my fellow panelists—a NAFTA supporter—reacted with rage: "It's comments like that that explain why people hate economists!") The job gains from increased exports or losses from import competition are tangible: You can actually see the people making the goods that foreigners buy, the workers whose factories were closed in the face of import competition. The other effects that economists talk about seem abstract. And yet if you accept the idea that the Fed has both a jobs target and the means to achieve it, you

{ 11 }

must conclude that changes in exports and imports have little effect on overall employment.

INVESTMENT AND THE TRADE BALANCE

Our second example, the relationship between foreign investment and trade balances, is equally troubling to business-people. Suppose that hundreds of multina-tional companies decide that a country is an ideal manufacturing site and start pouring billions of dollars a year into the country to build new plants. What happens to the country's trade balance? Business execu-tives, almost without exception, believe that the country will start to run trade surpluses. They are generally unconvinced by the economist's answer that such a country will *necessarily* run large trade *deficits*.

It's easy to see where the business-people's answer comes from. They think of their own companies and ask what would happen if capacity in their industries suddenly expanded. Clearly their companies would import less and export more. If the same story is played out in many industries, surely this would mean a shift toward a trade surplus for the economy as a whole.

The economist knows that just the opposite is true. Why? Because the balance of trade is part of the balance of payments, and the overall balance of payments of any country—the difference between its total sales to foreigners and its purchases from foreigners—must always be zero.[1] Of course, a country can run a trade deficit or surplus. That is, it can buy more goods from foreigners than it sells or vice versa. But that imbalance must always be matched by a corresponding imbalance in the capital account. A country that runs a trade deficit must be selling foreigners more assets than it buys; a country that runs a surplus must be a net investor abroad. When the United States buys Japanese automobiles, it must be selling something in return; it might be Boeing jets, but it could also be Rockefeller Center or, for that matter, Treasury bills. That is not just an opinion that economists hold; it is an unavoidable accounting truism.

So what happens when a country attracts a lot of foreign investment? With the inflow of capital, foreigners are acquiring more assets in that country than the country's residents are acquiring abroad. But that means, as a matter of sheer accounting, that the country's imports must, at the same time, exceed its exports. A country that attracts large capital inflows will necessarily run a trade deficit.

But that is just accounting. How does it happen in practice? When companies build plants, they will purchase some imported equipment. The investment inflow may spark a domestic boom, which leads to surging import demand. If the country has a floating exchange rate, the investment inflow may drive up the currency's value; if the country's exchange rate is fixed, the result may be inflation. Either scenario will tend to price the country's goods out of export markets and increase its imports. Whatever the channel, the outcome for the trade balance is not in doubt: Capital inflows must lead to trade deficits.

Consider, for example, Mexico's recent history. During the 1980s, nobody would invest in Mexico and the country ran a trade surplus. After 1989, foreign investment poured in amid new optimism about Mexico's prospects. Some of that money was spent on imported equipment for

Mexico's new factories. The rest fueled a
domestic boom, which sucked in imports
and caused the peso to become increasingly
overvalued. That, in turn, discouraged
exports and prompted many Mexican
consumers to purchase imported goods.
The result: Massive capital inflows were
matched by equally massive trade deficits.

Then came the peso crisis of December
1994. Once again, investors were trying
to get out of Mexico, not in, and the scenario
ran in reverse. A slumping economy reduced
the demand for imports, as did a newly
devalued peso. Meanwhile, Mexican exports
surged, helped by a weak currency. As any
economist could have predicted, the collapse
of foreign investment in Mexico has been

matched by an equal and opposite move of Mexican trade into surplus.

But like the proposition that expanded exports do not mean more employment, the necessary conclusion that countries attracting foreign investment typically run trade deficits sits poorly with business audiences. The specific ways in which foreign investment might worsen the trade balance seem questionable to them. Will investors really spend that much on imported equipment? How do we know that the currency will appreciate or that, if it does, exports will decrease and imports will increase? At the root of the businessperson's skepticism is the failure to understand the force of the accounting, which says that an inflow of

capital *must*—not *might*—be accompanied by
a trade deficit.

In each of the above examples, there is no
question that the economists are right and
the businesspeople are wrong. But why do
the arguments that economists find
compelling seem deeply implausible and
even counterintuitive to businesspeople?

There are two answers to that question.
The shallow answer is that the experiences
of business life do not generally teach practi-
tioners to look for the principles that underlie economists' arguments. The deeper
answer is that the kinds of feedback that typically arise in an individual business are both
weaker than and different from the kinds of
feedback that typically arise in the economy

as a whole. Let me analyze each of these answers in turn.

THE PARABLE OF THE PARALYZED CENTIPEDE

Every once in a while, a highly successful businessperson writes a book about what he or she has learned. Some of these books are memoirs: They tell the story of a career through anecdotes. Others are ambitious efforts to describe the principles on which the great person's success was based.

Almost without exception, the first kind of book is far more successful than the second, not only in terms of sales but also in terms of its reception among serious thinkers. Why?

Because a corporate leader succeeds not by developing a general theory of the corporation but by finding the particular product strategies or organizational innovations that work. There have been some business greats who have attempted to codify what they know, but such attempts have almost always been disappointing. George Soros's book told readers very little about how to be another George Soros; and many people have pointed out that Warren Buffett does not, in practice, invest the Warren Buffett Way. After all, a financial wizard makes a fortune not by enunciating general principles of financial markets but by perceiving particular, highly specific opportunities a bit faster than anyone else.

Indeed, great business executives often seem to do themselves harm when they try to formalize what they do, to write it down as a set of principles. They begin to behave as they think they are supposed to, whereas their previous success was based on intuition and a willingness to innovate. One is reminded of the old joke about the centipede who was asked how he managed to coordinate his 100 legs: He started thinking about it and could never walk properly again.

Yet even if a business leader may not be very good at formulating general theories or at explaining what he or she does, there are still those who believe that the business-person's ability to spot opportunities and solve problems in his or her own business

can be applied to the national economy.
After all, what the president of the United
States needs from his economic advisers is
not learned tracts but sound advice about
what to do next. Why isn't someone who has
shown consistently good judgment in
running a business likely to give the president good advice about running the country?
Because, in short, a country is not a large
company.

Many people have trouble grasping the
difference in complexity between even the
largest business and a national economy.
The U.S. economy employs 120 *million*
people, about 200 times as many as General
Motors, the largest employer in the United
States. Yet even this 200-to-1 ratio vastly

understates the difference in complexity
between the largest business organization
and the national economy. A mathematician
will tell us that the number of potential inter-
actions among a large group of people is
proportional to the square of their number.
Without getting too mystical, it is likely
that the U.S. economy is in some sense
not hundreds but tens of thousands of
times more complex than the biggest
corporation.

Moreover, there is a sense in which even
very large corporations are not all that
diverse. Most corporations are built around
a core competence: a particular technology
or an approach to a particular type of market.
As a result, even a huge corporation that

seems to be in many different businesses
tends to be unified by a central theme.

The U.S. economy, in contrast, is the
ultimate nightmare conglomerate, with tens
of thousands of utterly distinct lines of business, unified only because they happen to be
within the nation's borders. The experience
of a successful wheat farmer offers little
insight into what works in the computer
industry, which, in turn, is probably not a
very good guide to successful strategies for
a chain of restaurants.

How, then, can such a complex entity be
managed? A national economy must be
run on the basis of general principles, not
particular strategies. Consider, for example,
the question of tax policy. Responsible

governments do not impose taxes targeted at particular individuals or corporations or offer them special tax breaks. In fact, it is rarely a good idea for governments even to design tax policy to encourage or discourage particular industries. Instead, a good tax system obeys the broad principles developed by fiscal experts over the years—for example, neutrality between alternative investments, low marginal rates, and minimal discrimination between current and future consumption.

Why is that a problem for business-people? After all, there are many general principles that also underlie the sound management of a corporation: consistent accounting, clear lines of responsibility, and

so on. But many businesspeople have trouble
accepting the relatively hands-off role of a
wise economic policymaker. Business executives must be proactive. It is hard for someone used to that role to realize how much
more difficult—and less necessary—this
approach is for national economic policy.

Consider, for example, the question of
promoting key business areas. Only an
irresponsible CEO would not try to deter-
mine which new areas were essential to the
company's future; a CEO who left investment decisions entirely to individual managers running independent profit centers
would not be doing the job. But should a
government decide on a list of key industries
and then actively promote them? Quite aside

from economists' theoretical arguments
against industrial targeting, the simple fact
is that governments have a terrible track
record at judging which industries are
likely to be important. At various times,
governments have been convinced that
steel, nuclear power, synthetic fuels, semi-
conductor memories, and fifth-generation
computers were the wave of the future.
Of course, businesses make mistakes, too,
but they do not have the extraordinarily
low batting average of government because
great business leaders have a detailed
knowledge of and feel for their industries
that nobody—no matter how smart—can
have for a system as complex as a national
economy.

Still, the idea that the best economic management almost always consists of setting up a good framework and then leaving it alone doesn't make sense to businesspeople, whose instinct is, as Ross Perot put it, to "lift up the hood and get to work on the engine."

GOING BACK TO SCHOOL

In the scientific world, the syndrome known as "great man's disease" happens when a famous researcher in one field develops strong opinions about another field that he or she does not understand, such as a chemist who decides that he is an expert in medicine or a physicist who decides that he is an expert in cognitive science. The same

syndrome is apparent in some business
leaders who have been promoted to
economic advisers: They have trouble
accepting that they must go back to school
before they can make pronouncements in a
new field.

The general principles on which an economy must be run are different—not harder
to understand, but different—from those
that apply to a business. An executive who
is thoroughly comfortable with business
accounting does not automatically know
how to read national income accounts, which
measure different things and use different
concepts. Personnel management and labor
law are not the same thing; neither are
corporate financial control and monetary

policy. A business leader who wants to become an economic manager or expert must learn a new vocabulary and set of concepts, some of them unavoidably mathematical.

That is hard for a business leader, especially one who has been very successful, to accept. Imagine a person who has mastered the complexities of a huge industry, who has run a multibillion-dollar enterprise. Is such a person, whose advice on economic policy may well be sought, likely to respond by deciding to spend time reviewing the kind of material that is covered in freshman economics courses? Or is he or she more likely to assume that business experience is more than enough and that the unfamiliar words and concepts economists use are nothing but pretentious jargon?

Of course, in spite of the examples I gave earlier, many readers may still believe that the second response is the more sensible one. Why does economic analysis require different concepts, a completely different way of thinking, than running a business? To answer that question, I must turn to the deeper difference between good business thinking and good economic analysis.

The fundamental difference between business strategy and economic analysis is this: Even the largest business is a very open system; despite growing world trade, the U.S. economy is largely a closed system.

Businesspeople are not used to thinking
about closed systems; economists are.

Let me offer some noneconomic examples
to illustrate the difference between closed
and open systems. Consider solid waste.
Every year, the average American generates
about half a ton of solid waste that cannot be
recycled or burned. What happens to it?
In many communities, it is sent somewhere
else. My town requires that every resident
subscribe to a private disposal service but
provides no landfill site; the disposal service
pays a fee to some other community for the
right to dump our garbage. This means that
the garbage pickup fees are higher than they
would be if the town set aside a landfill site,
but the town government has made that

choice: It is willing to pay so that it won't have an unsightly dump within its borders.

For an individual town, that choice is feasible. But could every town and county in the United States make the same choice? Could we all decide to send our garbage somewhere else? Of course not (leaving aside the possibility of exporting garbage to the Third World). For the United States as a whole, the principle "garbage in, garbage out" applies literally. The country can make choices about where to bury its solid waste but not about whether to bury it at all. That is, in terms of solid waste disposal, the United States is more or less a closed system, even though each town is an open system.

That's a fairly obvious example. Here is
another, perhaps less obvious one. At one
point in my life, I was a "park-and-ride"
commuter: Every morning, I would drive to
a large parking garage and then take public
transportation downtown. Unfortunately,
the garage was not large enough. It consistently filled up, forcing late commuters to
continue driving all the way to work. I soon
learned, however, that I could always find a
parking space if I arrived by about 8:15.

In this case, each individual commuter
constituted an open system: He or she could
find a parking space by arriving early. But the
group of commuters as a whole could not do
the same. If everyone tried to get a space by
arriving earlier, the garage would only fill up

sooner! Commuters as a group constituted a closed system, at least as far as parking was concerned.

What does this have to do with business versus economics? Businesses—even very large corporations—are generally open systems. They can, for example, increase employment in all their divisions simultane- ously; they can increase investment across the board; they can seek a higher share of all their markets. Admittedly, the borders of the organization are not wide open. A company may find it difficult to expand rapidly because it cannot attract suitable workers fast enough or because it is unable to raise enough capital. An organization may find it even more difficult to contract, because it is reluctant to fire good employees. But we find nothing remarkable in a corporation whose market share doubles or halves in just a few years.

By contrast, a national economy—especially that of a very large country like the United States—is a closed system. Could all U.S. companies double their market shares over the next ten years?[2] Certainly not, no matter how much their managements improved. For one thing, in spite of growing world trade, more than 70% of U.S. employment and value-added is in industries, such as retail trade, that neither export nor face import competition. In those industries, one U.S. company can increase its market share only at the expense of another.

In industries that do enter into world trade, U.S. companies as a group can increase their market share, but they must do so by either increasing exports or driving down imports. Any increase in their market share would therefore mean a move into trade surplus; and, as we have already seen, a country that runs a trade surplus is necessarily a country that exports capital. A little arithmetic tells us that if the average U.S. company were to expand its share of the world market by as little as five percentage points, the United States, which is currently a net importer of capital from the rest of the world, would have to become a net exporter of capital on a scale never before seen. If you think this is an implausible scenario, you must also believe that U.S. companies cannot increase their combined share of the market by more than a percentage point or two, no matter how well run they are.

Businesspeople have trouble with economic analysis because they are accustomed to thinking about open systems. To return to our two examples, a businessperson looks at the jobs directly created by exports and sees those as the most important part of the story. He or she may acknowledge that higher employment leads to higher interest rates, but this seems an iffy, marginal concern. What the economist sees, however, is that employment is a closed system: Workers who gain jobs from increased exports, like park-and-ride commuters who secure parking spaces by arriving at the garage early, *must* gain those positions at someone else's expense.

And what about the effect of foreign investment on the trade balance? Again, the business executive looks at the direct effects of investment on competition in a particular industry; the effects of capital flows on exchange rates, prices, and so on do not seem particularly reliable or important. The economist knows, however, that the balance of payments is a closed system: The inflow of capital is always matched by the trade deficit, so any increase in that inflow *must* lead to an increase in that deficit.

FEEDBACKS IN BUSINESS
AND ECONOMICS

Another way of looking at the difference
between companies and economies may help
explain why great business executives are
often wrong about economics and why
certain economic ideas are more popular
with businesspeople than others: Open
systems like companies typically experience
a different kind of *feedback* than closed
systems like economies.

  This concept is best explained by hypo-
thetical example. Imagine a company that
has two main lines of business: widgets and
gizmos. Suppose that this company experiences unexpected growth in its sales of

widgets. How will that growth affect the sales of the company as a whole? Will increased widget sales end up helping or hurting the gizmo business? The answer in many cases will be that there is not much effect either way. The widget division will simply hire more workers, the company will raise more capital, and that will be that.

The story does not necessarily end here, of course. Expanded widget sales could either help or hurt the gizmo business in several ways. On one hand, a profitable widget business could help provide the cash flow that finances expansion in gizmos; or the experience gained from success in widgets may be transferable to gizmos; or the growth of the company may allow R&D efforts that benefit both divisions. On the other hand, rapid expansion may strain the company's resources, so that the growth of widgets may come to some extent at the gizmo division's expense. But such indirect effects of the growth of one part of the company on the success of the other are both ambiguous in principle and hard to judge in practice; feedbacks among different lines of business, whether they involve synergy or competition for resources, are often elusive.

By contrast, consider a national economy that finds one of its major exports growing rapidly. If that industry increases employment, it will typically do so at the expense of other industries. If the country does not at the same time reduce its inflows of capital,

the increase in one export must be matched
by a reduction in other exports or by an
increase in imports because of the balance
of payments accounting discussed earlier.
That is, there will most likely be strong
negative feedbacks from the growth of that
export to employment and exports in other
industries. Indeed, those negative feedbacks
will ordinarily be so strong that they will
more or less completely eliminate any
improvements in overall employment or
the trade balance. Why? Because employment and the balance of payments are closed
systems.

In the open-system world of business,
feedbacks are often weak and almost always
uncertain. In the closed-system world of

economics, feedbacks are often very strong
and very certain. But that is not the whole
difference. The feedbacks in the business
world are often positive; those in the world
of economic policy are usually, though not
always, negative.

Again, compare the effects of an expanding
line of business in a corporation and in a
national economy. Success in one line of business, which expands the company's financial,
technological, or marketing base, often helps
a company expand in other lines. That is, a
company that does well in one area may end
up hiring more people in other areas. But an
economy that produces and sells many goods
will normally find negative feedbacks among
economic sectors: Expansion of one industry

pulls resources of capital and labor away from other industries.

There are, in fact, examples of positive feedbacks in economics. They are often evident within a particular industry or group of related industries, especially if those industries are geographically concentrated. For example, the emergence of London as a financial center and of Hollywood as an entertainment center are clearly cases of positive feedback at work. However, such examples are usually limited to particular regions or industries; at the level of the national economy, negative feedback generally prevails. The reason should be obvious: An individual region or industry is a far more open system than the economy of the

United States as a whole, let alone the world
economy. An individual industry or group
of industries can attract workers from
other sectors of the economy; so if an individual industry does well, employment may
increase not only in that industry but also
in related industries, which may further
reinforce the success of the first industry,
and so on. Thus if one looks at a particular
industrial complex, one may well see positive
feedback at work. But for the economy as a
whole, those localized positive feedbacks
must be more than matched by negative
feedbacks elsewhere. Extra resources pulled
into any one industry or cluster of industries
must come from somewhere, which means
from other industries.

Businesspeople are not accustomed to or comfortable with the idea of a system in which there are strong negative feedbacks. In particular, they are not at all comfortable with the way in which effects that seem weak and uncertain from the point of view of an individual company or industry—such as the effect of reduced hiring on average wages or of increased foreign investment on the exchange rate—become crucially important when one adds up the impact of policies on the national economy as a whole.

WHAT'S A PRESIDENT TO DO?

In a society that respects business success, political leaders will inevitably—and rightly—seek the advice of business leaders on many issues, particularly those that involve money. All we can ask is that both the advisers and the advisees have a proper sense of what business success does and does not teach about economic policy.

In 1930, as the world slid into depression, John Maynard Keynes called for a massive monetary expansion to alleviate the crisis and pleaded for a policy based on economic analysis rather than on the advice of bankers committed to the gold standard or manufacturers who wanted to raise prices by restricting output. "For—though no one will believe it—economics is a technical and difficult subject."[3] Had his advice been followed, the worst ravages of the Depression might have been avoided.

Keynes was right: Economics is a difficult and technical subject. It is no harder to be a good economist than it is to be a good business executive. (In fact, it is probably easier, because the competition is less intense.) However, economics and business are not the same subject, and mastery of one does not ensure comprehension, let alone mastery, of the other. A successful business leader is no more likely to be an expert on economics than on military strategy.

The next time you hear businesspeople propounding their views about the economy, ask yourself, Have they taken the time to study this subject? Have they read what the experts write? If not, never mind how successful they have been in business. Ignore

them, because they probably have no idea
what they are talking about.

NOTES

1. There are actually two technical qualifications
to this statement. One of them involves what are
known as "unrequited transfers": gifts, foreign aid,
and so on. The other involves profits and interest
payments from past investments. These qualifications
do not change the main point.

2. Strictly speaking, one should talk of companies that produce in the United States. It is certainly
possible for companies based in the United States to
increase their world market share by acquiring foreign
subsidiaries.

3. "The Great Slump of 1930," reprinted in
Essays in Persuasion (New York: Norton, 1963).

ABOUT THIS AUTHOR

Paul Krugman is an op-ed columnist for the *New York Times* and a professor of economics and international affairs at Princeton University. He was awarded the Nobel Prize for Economics in 2008.

ALSO BY THIS AUTHOR

Harvard Business Review **Articles**
"Does Third World Growth Hurt First
World Prosperity?"
"How Fast Can the U.S. Economy Grow?"

CPSIA information can be obtained
at www.ICGtesting.com
Printed in the USA
BVHW070810091120
592842BV00004B/170